Top Giallo Movies

Alan Toner

ISBN: 9781697086515
Imprint: Independently published

Other Books By Alan Toner

True Ghost Stories
100 True Ghost Stories
200 True Ghost Stories
Famous Psychics
Hammer Horror Remembered
Hammer Horror Quiz Book
Hammer Horror Trivia
Haunted Objects
50 Celebrity Hauntings
UK UFOs
Creepy Doll Movies
Horror Stories
Horror Stories 2
Werewolf Nightmare
Haunted China

Contents

1. What is a Giallo Movie?

A giallo movie is a 20th-century Italian genre of film in which there is usually an unknown, shadowy, masked killer who stalks, and usually slaughters, a string of innocent people. In addition to copious amounts of blood and gore, not to mention the many trendy fashions sported by all kinds of jet-setting, beautiful people, the giallo movie usually incorporates detective and mystery elements. There may also be a sub plot or two thrown in for good measure (e.g. the hero's relationship with his wife, lover or boss etc.). In short, giallo is synonymous with "thriller".

The term "giallo" comes from a series of crime/mystery pulp novels entitled *Il Giallo Mondadori* (Mondadori Yellow), which were published by Mondadori, the largest publishing company in Italy, from 1929. Giallo means "yellow" in Italian, and so this colour was the trademark of this series of books. The series, with its eye-catching lurid paperback covers, usually featured translations of popular American crime fiction, although both European and Italian writers have started to be included more regularly.

Although Italy is considered to be the epicentre of giallo movies, there have also been many quality films of this genre produced by other countries like Spain, in addition to the French and English co-productions. Brian De Palma's 1980 classic *Dressed To Kill* is deemed by many to be the nearest America has got to producing an Italian-style giallo movie.

Going back even further, to 1960, Alfred Hitchcock's Psycho could be considered the movie that predates all the popular giallo films. Indeed, some would even say that all the giallo movies that followed were, in some way, inspired by Hitchcock's masterpiece.

A typical giallo film usually follows the same basic format: there is a pool of suspects, various clues are left, and the protagonist must discover the identity and motives of the killer over the course of the film. This is what differentiates a giallo from a slasher flick. In a slasher flick, we already know the killer's identity throughout the film, as he is normally a homicidal maniac, often with no motivation other than to mindlessly butcher as many victims as possible. But in a giallo film, the killer may be a deranged psycho with or without a motivation, and his identity is always kept a secret until the movie's conclusion. This adds a delicious mystery to the proceedings which all giallo buffs love. Beautiful women are usually the main targets of the black-gloved psychopathic killer in an archetypal giallo story. While most gialli involve a human killer, some also feature a supernatural element, which makes the story all the more gripping and fascinating.

Even though many of these giallo movies had low budgets and were, as such, often done quickly and sloppily, and with little consideration for character depth, they were, for all that, highly enjoyable little films. They were bloody, action-packed, colourful, set in some beautiful locations, and were packed with enough wild twists and turns to delight the heart of any giallo fan. They are also much sought after and treasured by all those who collect DVDs and Blu Rays in this genre. And when you add to this the fact that many of these giallo movies, both the classic and the more rare ones, have recently undergone gorgeous Hi Definition transfers to Blu Ray by such companies as Arrow Video, then it is obvious why the giallo genre continues to enjoy an ever-growing fan base all over the world.

So there you have it: an introductory definition of what exactly a giallo movie is. And now, in the following chapters, we will take a look at some top giallo movies, staring with a movie that is considered to be the very first giallo movie ever made.

2. The First Giallo Movie

The Girl Who Knew Too Much (1963) is often considered to be the very first giallo movie. Directed by Italian filmmaker Mario Bava and its title alluding to Alfred Hitchcock's *The Man Who Knew Too Much* (both the 1934 movie and the 1956 remake), it showcases the early link between gialli and Anglo-American crime stories. Also called *The Evil Eye* for its American release, the movie stars John Saxon as Dr. Marcello Bassi and Leticia Roman as Nora Davis.

The basic storyline centres on a young American woman named Nora who, whilst travelling in Rome in order to take care of an ailing family friend, witnesses a murder. When she reports it, neither the police nor Dr. Bassi believe her because no body has been found to substantiate her claim. When several more murders are committed, it is discovered that these are linked to decade-long string of killings of victims, all of whom are selected in alphabetical order.

It could be said that *The Girl Who Knew Too Much* laid the foundations for the typical giallo movie. What I mean by this is that the movie started the basic plot structure and elements which would be rehashed over and over again in future movies in the genre. Later on, these basic elements were expanded on with the introduction of sleaze and gruesome deaths in movies like *Blood and Black Lace* (1964), which was actually Mario Bava's second giallo film after *The Girl Who Knew Too Much*. It was also his last black and white film.

The movie bear some similarities to Agatha Christie's *The ABC Murders*, a Poirot story in which the murderer works his way through the alphabet as he slaughters people in order of their names. Although *The Girl Who Knew Too Much* it's not one of my favourite giallo movies, the film does have its moments, especially in regard to the inventive camerawork and lighting. In addition, there are moments of comedy peppered among all the deceit and murder. The movie also attested to the fact that Mario Bava can be equally effective in a modern setting as well as in a period setting. It also boasts a very palatable time-capsule travelogue view of Rome. However, having said all that, the movie is certainly no patch on Bava's later production, Blood and Black Lace (which is one of my all time favourite giallo movies), lacking that film's gorgeous colour, gruesome kills and in-your-face violence. Other weak spots in the movie were the annoying voice-over that insists on explaining what the images are making very clear by themselves, and performances that are uneven, especially in the supporting roles.

So if you are interested in checking out the wonderful world of Mario Bava, and want to explore the very beginnings of the giallo film, then *The Girl Who Knew Too Much* is certainly an ideal place to start.

3. Blood and Black Lace

Blood and Black Lace (1964) was Mario Bava's second giallo movie after *The Girl Who Knew Too Much* (1963). Having established a template for the giallo film with *The Girl Who Knew Too Much*, Mario Bava proceeded to solidify its tropes with *Blood and Black Lace*. In doing so he created one of the most influential films ever made - an Italian classic that would spearhead the giallo genre, provide a prototype for the slasher movie, and have an enormous effect on such top filmmakers as Dario Argento and Martin Scorsese.

The movie is considered one of the earliest and most influential of all gialli films, and served as a template for the "body count" slasher films of the 1980s. Tim Lucas said that the film inspired "legions of contemporary filmmakers, from Dario Argento to Martin Scorsese to Quentin Tarantino." In 2004, one of its sequences was voted No. 85 in "The 100 Scariest Movie Moments" by the Bravo TV network.

Mario Bava's ground-breaking murder-mystery, starring Cameron Mitchell and Eva Bartok, takes place around a fashion house called Christian Haute Couture where, one by one, women begin to be murdered by a person dressed in black and a creepy white mask, with a view to obtaining a scandal-revealing diary. A police inspector (Thomas Reiner) appears to have a list of suspects narrowed down. However, he soon realizes that his investigations will be constantly hindered by the many twists and turns in his path.

Being a former cinematographer, Bava certainly knew how to best present stunning and stylish visuals, a skill which very few other moviemakers could match. All the sets in this movie are just an aesthetic treat, flawlessly lighted with stark contrasts between darkness and light. The opening scene in particular is beautifully shot, with garish colours, and is wonderfully enhanced by that beating, jazzy music. Also, the level of violence in this movie was pretty strong for its time, the gruesome murder scenes still having the ability to shock even to this day. So if you love a piece of movie history pertaining to the giallo genre, then *Blood and Black Lace* is certainly an ideal choice.

All in all, *Blood and Black Lace* rates right up there as one of the best giallo movies ever made. It is visually stunning, has beautiful colours and lighting, an excellent music score, all the models are stunning, and of course we mustn't forget all those shockingly gruesome murders. It is, without doubt, one of Bava's best films. If you love giallo movies, then this is one you should definitely have in your collection.

4. The Bird With The Crystal Plumage

Now we come to what is, without doubt, my all time favourite giallo movie: *The Bird With The Crystal Plumage* (1970). Really, there are so many superlatives I could utter about this masterpiece of a film. For me, it is the perfect giallo movie.

Made in 1970 and directed by Dario Argento, *The Bird With The Crystal Plumage* (Italian: *L'uccello dalle piume di cristallo*) tells the story of Sam Dalmas (Tony Musante), an American writer living in Rome with his model girlfriend Giulia (played by the gorgeous Suzy Kendall). Experiencing a bad case of writer's block, he decides to return to the USA. However, his intentions are put on hold when he witnesses the attempted murder of the female owner of an art gallery. Unfortunately, Sam is unable to intervene, as he is trapped between two glass doors. The person responsible for this crime is apparently a serial killer hunting young girls, and Sam will stop at nothing to find out who the killer is. However, the hunter soon becomes the hunted, as the crazed killer starts to stalk Sam and his girlfriend.

In his directorial debut, Argento does a brilliant job with this, the movie that made him a European sensation. He consummately and flawlessly entertains and thrills both critics and movie buffs alike with his elegant use of camerawork, lighting and shadows, colours and editing, giving this film a wonderfully garish style. In addition, he presents us with a highly gripping and unpredictable plotline that never flags for one single minute. Argento wrote the script with Fredric Brown's novel *The Screaming Mimi* in mind. Another terrific Argento trademark is the music. Ennio Morricone's hauntingly beautiful score is nothing short of fantastic.

Not only was the movie a huge commercial success, but it was also nominated for an Edgar Allan Poe award for best motion picture in 1971, an honour truly deserved. Moreover, the movie has become a much-revisited reference for all filmmakers and movie buffs, and was placed 272nd in Empire magazine's "500 Greatest Movies of All Time" list.

A lot of people, included myself, have wondered exactly what significance does the title *The Bird With The Crystal Plumage* have in relation to the film. Well, the title refers to a very rare species of bird, which calls in the background when the mysterious killer phones and threatens the hero. So the bird's sound represents a clue for locating his flat.

In addition to the sheer brilliance of Dario Argento's directing, the movie boasts a brilliant cast. Tony Musante is fantastic as the film's glamour-boy hero turned civilian investigator. Enrico Maria Salerno also does a fine job in the role of Inspector Morosini. And Suzy Kendall is, of course, equally superb as the hero's glamorous damsel-in-distress girlfriend.

There some differences between the British BFFC-18 DVD version and the uncut version of the movie. The DVD is slightly censored, as three scenes of the killer attacking two women were cut.

When the killer is finally revealed at the end of the

movie, it really is quite a jaw-dropping and clever moment, and one that you certainly won't have seen coming.

All in all, *The Bird With The Crystal Plumage* is a truly top-notch film, and a must-see not just for fans of Argento's work, but also for those seeking a gripping thriller or well-constructed murder mystery. It is an authentic giallo, like only a real Italian master of his craft can deliver them, and boy, does Argento deliver here!

5. A Bay of Blood

Here's a little question for you: what is much worse and much more horrifying than having one deranged serial killer in a movie? Well, having the ENTIRE cast as deranged serial killers! And this is exactly what happens in the 1971 movie *A Bay of Blood*. All bets are off as the people in this movie get mercilessly and indiscriminately slaughtered left, right and centre.

Often considered to be Mario Bava's most influential film, *A Bay of Blood* (or *Twitch of the Death Nerve*) is also regarded by most fans of the genre as the grandfather of the modern slasher film, sharing the same premise as Friday The 13th (1980) in that teenagers are slaughtered near a stretch of water. Indeed, two of the killings in Bava's movie are taken directly from two killings in *Friday The 13th Part II.*

Bay of Blood has a very unique concept that none of its imitators have successfully copied: the concept of people being murdered one by one, and not by just one killer but by several, in the most gruesome ways imaginable, and with a smattering of super dry black comedy thrown in for good measure. This movie is definitely one of the most way out, crazy kill-fest flicks I have ever seen, and is the type of movie that shuns all gradual character build-up and fleshing out – characters you want to root for, in other words – in favour of a straight in-your-face murder spree.

11

Now there are some who may not like this kind of story, especially those who prefer the more traditional one-killer giallo movie with well-rounded characters and a whodunit plot. However, there are also those who welcome this touch of insane originality in a movie featuring multiple killers in one grand, unrelenting blood bath. And if ever there was a movie of the latter variety, then *Bay of Blood* is certainly it.

The movie opens with a scenario involving a wheelchair-bound and wealthy countess, who owns the lands of a disputed bay. She is cold-bloodedly hanged by a mysterious assailant immersed in shadow (reminiscent of a Hitchcock scene). That assailant turns out to be her husband, and he is immediately killed (what goes around comes around, eh?). The crime scene is falsified to make it look as if the old woman has taken her own life. Later on, two young couples are brutally murdered in the titular bay. The inheritors of the fortune of the countess all then strive to get their greedy hands on the place, and resort to heinously murdering each other through any means possible, hence setting off a continuous bloodbath in the area.

When you really analyse the movie, you find that there's something quite stealthy and unique about Mario Bava's approach to the intentionally confusing plot. Throughout the maze-like story line, we jump from one character to the next, having scant time to get to know the people in the movie to care enough for them. When they are killed, their deaths suddenly take on a surprisingly contemporary aspect. This twist represents a rather bold, risky approach to the conventional slasher flick, but to judge by the many favourable reviews of this movie, coupled with the cult status it has generated with fans over the years, it's an approach that seems to have paid off really well.

One gimmick used to promote the movie that was kind of reminiscent of the kind of gimmicks that William Castle would employ in his movies was that every ticket holder was required to pass through The Final Warning Station, where a theatre worker warned you, face to face, that this may be the last 'shock' film you will ever want to see.

A Bay Of Blood was such a pivotal movie in the history of screen horror, perhaps as significant as Hitchcock's classic *Psycho*. Bava's film signalled the moment where giallo cinema overspilled into slasher horror, with *A Bay Of Blood's* whodunit premise becoming secondary to another, equally enthralling diversion: who was going to die next, and just how horrible would that death be?

As all character motivation or logic is thrown completely out of the window here, what sets *Bay of Blood* apart from *Friday The 13th* and similar slasher movies is Bava's unique visual style, coupled with a touch of wry humour and a heavy jazzy score. Bava's presentation is absolutely spot on, with intermittent atmospheric interludes utilising the natural features of the landscape, from slow pans across the horizon, focus pulls through the foliage, and the swift zooming in and out of each gruesome murder.

I won't say too much about the ending of *Bay of Blood*, as I would not want to spoil this punch-in-gut twist for you. Suffice to say that it does have a rather cheeky slant to it and, as such, one that you will either love or loathe. Anyway, having said that, *A Bay of Blood* is definitely a movie that you should add to your collection, because for all its sheer craziness and shallow-character slaughtering and jarring scene settings, the movie has an undoubted place in slasher flick history as a highly significant and influential piece of film making.

6. Don't Torture A Duckling

Don't Torture A Duckling (1972) has often been described by Lucio Fulci, in many interviews, as his most personal favourite out of all the movies he has ever directed. Indeed, the film has gained something of a reputation over the years as being his masterpiece, and it is certainly hard to dispute this rating.

The movie tells the story of a series of child murders, all young boys, in a parochial village in Southern Italy. It is a village rife in superstition and a deep mistrust of outsiders. A local witch, with a reputation for dabbling in the black arts, immediately becomes the prime suspect in the killings. Another suspect is a rather dopey, perverted farmhand that loves spying on prostitutes. A journalist, Andrea (Tomas Milian), and a rich sophisticate from the city, Patrizia (Barbara Bouchet), get sucked into the murder mystery. Before the identity of the killer is revealed, deeper mysteries in the village will generate yet more horrific violence and local panic. What initially appears to be a fairly conventional set-up for a giallo proceeds to combine religion, superstition and a memorable cast of eccentric characters into a gripping, well-constructed film.

In true exploitation style, the movie also has some pretty luscious women and bloody slayings. Then there is the very well paced, intricate plot, offering an ample number of twists and turns to keep you guessing right till the very end. And there are some parts in the movie that are quite disturbing. For instance, an adult woman sexually teases a 12-year-old boy. And young kids are shown smoking in a manner that would be deemed quite unacceptable today. Such lurid moments clearly show how Fulci could occasionally totter on the border between the decadent and the entertaining.

The film also features a couple of scenes of grisly violence, albeit minimal, for which Fulci would later become famous, including a brutal chain-whipping sequence, which would later be repeated in *The Beyond* (1980). In common with many giallo movies, *Don't Torture A Duckling's* colourful title bears little relevance to the main plot or its grisly overtones; rather, the name is derived from a small plot detail.

All in all, *Don't Torture A Duckling* is extremely good viewing for all giallo and Fulci fans. It's a movie that relies more on the suspense and atmosphere value than the blood and gore element. Even though anybody who is well versed in how giallo movies play out will probably guess the killer within the first twenty minutes, that is not much of a problem, and certainly doesn't detract from the general entertainment value of this film.

7. The Cat o' Nine Tails

I have to admit that *Cat o' Nine Tails* (1971), even though it has been highly rated in the giallo genre by some fans, is definitely not one of my favourite giallo movies. In fact, to be perfectly honest, I was bored sick with it. Indeed, even Dario Argento himself has gone on record as saying that the movie is the least favourite of his own work. Even so, whilst the movie is generally regarded as a relatively minor early work of his, it is still his most popular video rental in his native Italy.

Basically, *Cat o' Nine Tails* (Italian: *Il Gatto A Nove Code*) is a kind of murder mystery reminiscent of the kind both Alfred Hitchcock and Agatha Christie became famous for. The main problem with the movie is that it fails to deliver all the usual Argento set pieces for which he has become so famous: gratuitous violence, stunning camera-work, bloody slaughters, insane story-lines, brutality towards women, and so on. So it's small wonder that many Argento fans were sorely disappointed with this film. Anyway, on to the basic storyline.

Karl Malden (of *The Streets of San Franciso* fame) portrays a crossword-puzzle-writing blind man who joins forces with a reporter (James Franciscus) to catch a killer with an extra chromosome. In so doing, both become targets of the killer. Most of the action occurs at a research hospital, where the killer seeks to cover up the original crime with a

16

string of more murders.

Although it is the second film in Argento's "Animal Trilogy" (which began with *The Bird with the Crystal Plumage* and ended with *Four Flies on Grey Velvet*), the metaphorical phrase "cat o' nine tails" does not directly refer to a literal cat, nor to a literal multi-tailed whip; instead, it refers to the nine separate leads that the protagonists follow in their endeavours to solve a murder. There is, however, one scene in the movie, which takes place in a cemetery, where an actual cat is mentioned by the characters. And while there are no actual moggies in the movie, there is a fair amount of cat burglary, plus a climactic catfight across the tiles of a rooftop. And that's your lot, as far as the inclusion of cats are concerned in this movie.

Running to 112 minutes, *Cat o' Nine Tails* is one of the only Argento films that outstays its welcome. As already implied, I was so disappointed with this movie, especially after being utterly thrilled and entertained by the brilliant *The Bird With The Crystal Plumage*. Needless to say, it's one that I immediately decided would have no place in my Blu Ray collection.

8. Four Flies On Grey Velvet

Four Flies On Grey Velvet ((Italian: *4 Mosche Di Velluto Grigio*) is the third movie in Dario Argento's "Animal Trilogy", the first two having been *The Bird With The Crystal Plumage* (1970) and *The Cat o' Nine Tails* (1971).

Based on a story by Luigi Cozzi (who was also the assistant director) and released in 1972, the movie concerns a musician called Roberto Tobias (Michael Brandon), a drummer in a rock band, who is not only being plagued by strange phone calls, but is also being followed by a mysterious man in dark sunglasses. One night, in a derelict opera house, Tobias manages to catch up with his stalker and tries to get him to talk, but in the ensuing struggle he accidentally stabs the man, who falls from the stage to the floor. Then, suddenly, a spotlight is turned on, and Tobias is photographed in the crime scene by a masked person on a theatre box. Tobias runs away, but that certainly isn't the end of his torment, for the following day he receives an envelope containing photos of him killing the man. Someone is murdering all his friends, and trying to pin the blame on him. But is everything really as it seems?

Four Flies On Grey Velvet is definitely one of Argento's strangest films, (a foretaste of the equally strange but much more enjoyable and colourful *Suspiria*). Also, it's a movie that I don't really rate as being one of his best. It becomes quite slow-paced and dull, especially around the middle part.

However, it does have some excellent technical style and impressive effects throughout. It also boasts a pounding rock score by Ennio Morricone, in addition to a young Michael Brandon before he became famous as the star of the TV series *Dempsey and Makepeace.*

But getting back to the negatives, I deemed the script to be, on the whole, pretty weak. Also, I found the ending to be a complete let down, derivative, and somewhat rushed. But I won't reveal too much here, as you will have to see the film yourself to form your own opinion.

9. What Have You Done To Solange?

What Have You Done To Solange? (Italian: *Cosa avete fatto a Solange?*) is a 1972 Italian/West German production set in a Catholic girls' school in Britain. It is supposedly based on one of Edgar Wallace's books, namely *The Clue of the New Pin*. Directed by Massimo Dallamano and starring Fabio Testi, Karin Baal, Joachim Fuchsberger, Cristina Galbó, and Camille Keaton, the storyline concerns a string of brutal killings at the school where a young student has gone missing.

Whilst in a boat having sex with the school's hunky Italian gym teacher, Enrico (Fabio Testi), a young woman (who is also the coach's 18-year-old student) witnesses a man with a knife stabbing another woman in the woods on the nearby shore. Enrico persuades his mistress not to reveal what she saw, especially after it appears that the murdered victim was one of her classmates.

Later on, Enrico's mistress is murdered in her bathroom. Police suspicion immediately falls on the teacher, who subsequently confesses his affair to his sexually frustrated wife with a view to getting her help to clear his name (in the familiar style of a Hitchcock protagonist). Amid all of this, other women begin to go missing at the school. Enrico is eventually cleared when a link is made by the later murders:

the victims all had seen a local clergyman and had befriended a young woman (Solange) who began attending the school the previous semester, but then had mysteriously gone missing.

Enrico's investigation ultimately leads to the existence of a decadent secret club of college girls to which both his mistress and the other murder victims belonged. The police further discover that the priest to whom some of the victims had spoken was not a real priest at all; he was instead Solange's father, an affluent businessman.

Compared to some giallo movies, *What Have You Done To Solange?* is quite a heavy watch. Teenage girls are sexually abused, the killings are horrific (albeit not as bloody as in some giallo movies), and moral boundaries are breached in such a way as to make you feel considerably uncomfortable. And we get the typical giallo shots of the killer's black-gloved hands as they kill. But for all those questionable extremes, the film is very well constructed and directed, has strong characters, copious nudity, some stunningly colourful imagery, and is rife with some great twists and layers of complexity that will keep you hooked right to the very end. It also has a fantastically haunting musical score by Ennio Morricone.

Given all these engaging qualities, it is a movie that you should definitely add to your giallo collection.

21

10. Your Vice Is A Locked Room, And Only I Have The Key

This rather lengthily titled movie, directed by Sergio Martino and released in 1972, follows the story of a career-fading, alcoholic writer, Oliviero Rouvigny (Luigi Pistilli) and his patiently enduring wife, Irina (Anita Strindberg), as they live out their gloomy lives in an old decrepit mansion that once belonged to his mother. To alleviate his boredom, Oliviero holds debauched parties for local hippies, during which he constantly belittles his wife in front of all the guests.

When his mistress, a young student, is found murdered, all suspicion falls on Oliviero. When he discovers the dead body of the family's maid on the premises, he takes steps to conceal it in order to avoid further suspicion.

As nobody has any clue on exactly who the murderer is, Oliviero's anxiety begins to mount, resulting in more ill treatment of his wife. When Oliviero's niece Floriana (Fenech) suddenly arrives for a visit, his problems are compounded. Irina finds solace in Floriana's arms and bed, and the two decide to concoct a plan to deal with Oliviero.

Your Vice Is a Locked Room and Only I Have the Key was Martino's fourth giallo film. The title of the film is a reference to his first one, *The Strange Vice of Mrs. Wardh*

(*Lo Strano Vizio della Signora Wardh*, 1971), in which the killer leaves the phrase as a note to his victim. The victim in that film was played by Fenech. The film has been released under several alternate titles, including *Gently Before She Dies*, *Eye of the Black Cat* and *Excite Me*!

The movie is quite a stylistic and engrossing treat. The collaboration of Martino, cinematographer Giancarlo Ferrando and composer Bruno Nicolai ensures that the visual and audible aspects of the movie are the best they can possibly be. Also, the malevolent atmosphere that pervades the storyline does much to create an overwhelming sense of suspense and tension that gradually builds to an exciting, if somewhat predictable, conclusion. The heavy use of darkness and shadow also adds to the general ambience of fear and unease.

Another well-executed aspect of the movie is the intermittent flash of the baleful cat's eyes during certain scenes, which becomes more frequent as the film rushes to its climax. The almost hypnotic glare of the snarling and vicious cat could be taken as a twofold symbol of the mental breakdowns of the characters, and the deteriorating relationship between Oliviero and Irina. Actually, the use of the feline element is a clear homage to Edgar Allan Poe's classic short story, *The Black Cat*. Indeed, even the opening credits acknowledge this influence.

11. Short Night of the Glass Dolls

First released as *La Corta notte delle bambole di vetro* in Italy, *Short Night of the Glass Dolls* (1971) is set amid the Cold War and tells the story of American reporter Gregory Moore (Jean Sorel), whose corpse is found in a Prague plaza and brought to the local morgue. However, Moore is not really dead, but is actually trapped alive in his dead body. As his mind desperately tries to recall both how he ended up in the morgue, and how the mysterious disappearance of his beautiful girlfriend Mira (Barbara Bach) sparked off a sinister conspiracy of depravity, the clock is ticking away towards Moore's impending autopsy doom.

The movie is predominantly told through Moore's flashbacks from the morgue, where an old friend of his is trying to revive him because he believes something is wrong with the body, on account of the fact that rigor mortis has not set in.

The next hour of the movie runs at a very slow pace. Through flashbacks, we learn that Moore's girlfriend disappears at a party without a trace. Consequently, Moore then embarks on his own investigation when the Prague police (whose attire is reminiscent of the Gestapo) prove to be of little help. His investigation leads him from one place to the next, and he eventually discovers that Mira is not the only missing girl in Prague.

As he gets nearer to the truth about the missing girls, someone tries to thwart both his own efforts and those of the people who are assisting him. Their investigation leads them to a strange high profile private club, whose affluent members indulge in odd ritualistic orgies and arcane dark rites. The whole thing smacks of some giant conspiracy – perhaps a Satanic one? I won't reveal too much about the twist ending; suffice to say that it is both superb and horrific.

Short Night of the Glass Dolls is a very different kind of giallo film, mainly because of the rather interminable pace, being both too short on incident and seriously lacking in any real edge-of-seat thrills and chills. Though the premise is quite strong, it still lacks the lurid and brutal killings that have become so emblematic of the giallo genre. In some ways, the movie has parallels to some of the work of Roman Polanski, like *Rosemary's Baby* (1968) and *The Tenant* (1976). It also bears disturbing similarities to movies that deal with catalepsy, like *The Premature Burial* (1962), wherein the mind is still very much alive whilst the body bears all the outwards signs that the person is completely dead.

To sum up, *Short Night of the Glass Dolls* left me feeling extremely disappointed and, as such, disqualified it from a place in my giallo movie collection.

12. Torso

Torso (1973) is one of my all time favourite giallo movies, not least that it stars one of my favourite horror movie actresses: the lovely Suzy Kendall (*The Bird With The Crystal Plumage, Spasmo* etc.). In addition, the movie has a damn good plot, with plenty of thrills, chills and gruesome murders to delight the heart of any true giallo flick fan. To top it all, the film has a damn good twist too.

Torso (original title *I Corpi Presentano Tracce di Violenza Carnale*) is set in Perugia and tells the story of a group of gorgeous young Italian co-eds who become terrified when their friends start getting bumped off by a brutal slasher, who has a horrific predilection for strangling, stabbing and fondling the naked bodies of his victims. His gruesome calling card is a red-and-black scarf left at each murder scene. Four of the girls take refuge in a villa in a small, picturesque village in an attempt to escape all the atrocities committed on campus. But the crazed murderer has followed them there, and is hell bent on killing them off, one by one.

In many ways, Torso is quite an explicit, in-your-face movie. All the murders are carried out with extreme sadism, and there is even a touch of misogyny in the killer's actions. There is also a small lesbian subplot involving two of the girls, although nothing particularly explicit is shown. No male nudity though. Whilst the movie could be condemned by some as a kind of sleazy, exploitation flick, I think that it still holds up as a very enjoyable and well-constructed giallo film, with great photography and a decent cast. I love the way the movie toys with the audience's expectations, scattering red herrings here and there. And, of course, being a HUGE fan of the gorgeous Suzy Kendall, I have to say that her heroine, Jane, comes across as being extremely resourceful and intelligent. She really is the icing on the cake in this brilliant movie. And what she witnesses in the isolated villa at the horrific climax of the movie . . . Well, I won't spoil it for you by divulging any more. You'll just have to go see it yourself to see what I mean.

Eli Roth, director of such grisly horror movies as *Hostel* and *Green Inferno*, is a big fan of *Torso*, and even provides an introduction to the movie on the Blue Underground Blu Ray.

Despite its attention-grabbing title, *Torso* is not as violent on a visceral level as most contemporary horror films. However, its reputation as a good, solid giallo movie is secured because the grisly scenes leave room for the viewer's imagination do most of the work. It also has one of the most gripping climaxes I have ever seen in a giallo movie. In addition, the movie is replete in great atmosphere, which is always an essential thing for me with movies of this kind. The location settings, particularly the dark bridge underpass and mist-shrouded forest, make for creepy places for the victims to meet their grisly ends. To top it all, the outstanding music score by Guido De Angelis and Maurizio De Angelis enhances the enjoyability factor of this gripping thriller.

Torso is Sergio Martino's most graphic giallo. And the part where the killer stalks a woman in the woods is certainly

Torso's most memorable death scene.

If I were to compile a Top 10 list of my all time favourite giallo movies, *Torso* would definitely be right near the top. It's a movie with a high rewatchability factor, and one that I can't recommend enough.

13. A Blade in the Dark

A Blade In The Dark (Italian title: *La casa con la scala nel buio, lit. 'The House with the Dark Staircase'*) is a 1983 Italian giallo movie directed by Lamberto Bava. Initially, the movie was planned to be shown on television as a two-hour feature split into four parts, culminating in a murder scene. However, it was deemed to explicit for TV by the Italian censors, and so the script was re-edited into a feature film.

The story centres on Bruno (Andrea Occhipinti), a composer working on a musical score for a horror film. To get him in the right mood, his director arranges for him to stay in a large, secluded villa. It is a place that is shrouded in mystery, for nobody knows what happened to the previous tenant. Somewhat perturbed by the place, Bruno invites his girlfriend to visit. However, living there soon becomes even more perturbing when the former tenant's beautiful friends start dying, one after the other, at the hands of a razor-wielding slasher. And as if all that isn't unsettling enough, there is a strange next-door neighbour who becomes a key suspect in the murders.

The most notable failing of this generally well-told mystery is that it is marred by some truly awful dubbing, not to mention a rather dodgy translation. This turns what should have been darkly atmospheric scenes into pathetic comedy. Some plot devices are laughably weak, and there are a few red herrings that hinge on characters engaging in some pretty far-fetched behaviour. However, those failings aside, there are enough shocks and scares along the way to satisfy the average giallo buff, and Bava certainly knows to ratchet up the tension in parts.

14. The Perfume of the Lady In Black

The Perfume of the Lady In Black (Italian: *Il Profumo Della Signora In Nero*) is a 1974 giallo film, with horror elements, directed by Francesco Barilli. It is one of the most beautifully shot giallo movies ever, with blue being a prominent colour in everyone's living quarters. The movie also exhibits a world where different hues and shades of purple and pink are plentiful. And there is a strong floral theme to both the decoration of apartments and the actors' attire, with at least one of the characters also having a floral name. Plus, of course, the movie has a wonderfully ornate title.

Italian giallo buffs will instantly recognise the movie's rather complex, winding plot, its operatic melodrama, and the explicit sexuality and blood spilling that increases as the movie progresses. But for all that, the movie is still quite a slow burner and, as such, may not appeal to all those viewers who like their giallo movies to be fast and furious and replete with bloody killings.

The story centres on an attractive blonde (the kind you'd see in a Hitchcock movie), who begins to hallucinate (or does she?) images from her childhood that revolve around a lady in black, and of strangers who follow her everywhere. The role features Mimsy Farmer, who plays a talented chemist, Silvia, whose commitment to her job sparks tension in her relationship with her boyfriend (Maurizio Bonuglia), who doesn't seem to have much affection for her anyway. In fact, most of her friends and neighbours treat her with similar chameleon-like behaviour. For example, in one scene, they cajole her into a sitting with a medium, and seem to get a kick out of it when the experience causes her emotional distress. But as the movie plods on, it soon becomes clear that Silvia isn't entirely the victim here, for as she's visited by ghosts from the past, including herself at a younger age, it's revealed that she was behind a horrible crime, and that those malevolent tendencies may not have disappeared entirely.

In the tradition of most giallo horrors, the emphasis is more on the aesthetic than the actual storyline. The movie has all the usual elements of the supernatural and psychosis, as Silvia's belief that she's being made the target of some kind of witchcraft blends with her hallucinations, which could be either suppressed memories, are realities being perpetrated against her by some unidentified enemy, or are the result of something more unearthly. And the bloody body count, which does not come until quite later on in the movie and which runs alongside her mysterious and malevolent psychotic episodes is a good unique spin on the popular Italian giallo genre. What is particularly unsettling about the film is how hard it is to completely understand what's going on, or why.

The ending is predictable, but still utterly breathtaking and brutal, and makes little sense. Some viewers, though, would see this as just all part of the fun of this rather weird, wonderfully colourful giallo flick.

15. The Case of the Scorpion's Tale

Filmed mostly in Greece, *The Case of the Scorpion's Tail* (Italian: *La coda dello scorpione / Tail of the Scorpion*) is a 1971 Italian giallo movie directed by Sergio Martino (a regular name in this genre) and produced by Luciano Martino.

Co-written by Ernesto Gastaldi and Eduardo Maria Brochero, the story opens with a widow named Lisa (Ida Galli) who inherits one million dollars when her insured husband dies in a freak plane crash. As suspicion about her possible involvement in her husband's death grows, and she attempts to flee to a retreat with her secret lover, Lisa is horrifically slashed to death by an unknown assailant, and the money is stolen (shades of *Psycho* here as the story focuses on a particular protagonist for the first act of the movie before she shockingly becomes an unexpected murder victim and the focus switches to another character for the remainder of the film).

An insurance investigator (George Hilton) and his female journalist lover (Anita Strindberg), take on the case, sniffing out any irregularities as they try to find out exactly who is murdering anybody who had links with the late widow, and why. The only key to the mystery is a strange gold cufflink. The titular piece of evidence, the Scorpion's Tail itself, doesn't come into play until more than 50 minutes into the run time. Similar to many other gialli with animals in the title, the scorpion and its tail are a MacGuffin within a MacGuffin (it was the late, great Alfred Hitchcock who coined the phrase "MacGuffin).

The movie has quite a complex plot, with plenty of red herrings. It's a kind of generic story about people killing for money and letting their greed run wild. However, the main thing that spoiled this movie for me was that the story unfortunately lacked those extra special sexual and psychological elements essential to a good, memorable giallo flick. Instead, the plot unfolds as more of a routine, unsensational mystery, and even though the characters are well fleshed out, their fates hinge solely on the plot rather than on their own personal traits and flaws. Also, the pace of the story does tend to slow down a bit after the first murder. Moreover, the blood and gore effects aren't really anything to write home about (the blood looks more like red paint), and the solution, which most won't actually see coming, is not the most original of endings.

Those few flaws aside, the movie does have some redeeming features, as the suave George Hilton and the luscious Anita Strindberg do make quite an engaging couple, and the story does venture to breach some boundaries as it strives to entertain audiences (the first slashing comes as quite a shock). Also, the cinematography is very good, and the movie switches from scene to scene very easily. This bears testament to just how consummate and talented a director Sergio Martino is. Well, after all, he did make five giallo movies in a row, so obviously he knows his stuff.

So if you are just a simple mystery story fan, and are not too bothered about the lack of any real, strong, traditional giallo tropes, then you should be fairly satisfied with this movie.

16. Hatchet For The Honeymoon

Hatchet for the Honeymoon (Italian: *Il Rosso Segno Della Follia*, lit. '*The Red Sign of Madness*') is a 1970 giallo film directed by Mario Bava and starring Stephen Forsyth, Dagmar Lassander, Laura Betti, and Femi Benussi. It is a rather unique giallo movie in that it contains strong supernatural elements too, which, I must say, blend in quite well with the murder aspects.

The storyline, set in Paris, centres on the young manager of a bridal dress factory, John Harrington (Stephen Forsyth), who, in a narrative voiceover, claims to be prone to the Oedipus Complex. His psychosis, sparked off when, as a kid, he witnessed the brutal slaying of her mother during her wedding night, starts driving him to brutally murdering women dressed in their bridal gowns, using not a hatchet but a shiny meat cleaver. This is the giallo part that runs parallel to the supernatural element of Harrington's overbearing wife, whom he also murders, repeatedly coming back from the dead to haunt him, threatening to make him even more screwy than he already is. Actually, such giallo and the supernatural subgenres were of huge appeal to Bava, who touched on them in many of his other films.

Hatchet for the Honeymoon appears to have had a strong influence on *American Psycho* (2000), which was directed by Mary Harron and was based on the notorious Bret Easton Ellis novel of the same name. Both movies do succeed in revealing the utter decadence of the wealthy through the wicked actions of a charismatic but ultimately narcissistic and psychotic individual. Indeed, the John Harrington character appears to be the precursor to the character of Patrick Bateman (played by Christian Bale in American Psycho). Just like Bateman, Harrington is all too aware that he is insane. Initially, his psychosis troubles him somewhat, but he soon becomes amused by it, allowing it free reign as he sets about embarking on his vicious killing spree.

Easily alternating from the linear plot of Harrington lurking in the shadows amongst his mannequins, to a string of surreal set pieces, this style of storytelling doesn't disrupt the narrative too much, and this is a great strength of the movie for which Bava must be commended. With its strong Freudian subtexts, its display of hallucinatory-like images, and its presentation of intense emotional responses to childhood traumas, the narrative structure of Hatchet for the Honeymoon also has a strong Gothic element. Even the setting for John's home and business, an elegant French villa near Paris, resembles a castle as foreboding as Dracula's.

Many have opined that *Hatchet for a Honeymoon* is not one of Bava's best movies, but I would tend to disagree. On the contrary, I think it's one of his best, and I especially love the way he blends in the ghostly elements with the giallo ones, making it quite a bizarre, unique movie in the genre. The colourful cinematography is also beautifully shot, and really captures the mood of the late sixties. Another enjoyable aspect is the touch of black humour that Bava injects into the movie, even at the risk of ridiculing his main character, as he has Harrington dressing up in a bridal veil to butcher his victims. And, of course, Stephen Forsyth is just brilliant in the role of the demented bridal house boss.

If you fancy a giallo movie that is a little different, I would highly recommend you check out *Hatchet for a Honeymoon*. It's a real ghost-meets-the-hatchet-killer fun ride.

17. A Lizard in a Woman's Skin

A Lizard in a Woman's Skin (Italian: *Una Lucertola Con La Pelle Di Donna*) is a 1971 Italian giallo film directed by Lucio Fulci. The film was released in France as Carole, and was later re-released in the US as Schizoid.

The movie is set in London and tells the story of politician's daughter Carol Hammond (Florinda Bolkan), who lives in a grand building with her husband, Frank Hammond, and her stepdaughter, Joan Hammond. Carol starts experiencing a succession of lurid, psychedelic nightmares in which decadent sex orgies and LSD usage feature. In the dream, she finds herself committing a brutal murder, and then awakens to a real-life criminal investigation into the murder of her neighbour. Inspector Corvin (Stanley Baker) and his partner, Sgt. Brandon, are assigned to investigate. All the evidence points to Carol, but was it all just a dream, or did the murder actually happen?

The film could be described as a kind of hallucinatory psychodrama, and is particularly notorious for a certain graphic scene in which Mrs. Hammond opens the door to a room filled with dogs that are being experimented on. The dogs are sliced open, fully exposing their still pulsating hearts and innards. The scene was so explicit and stomach-churning that a few of the crew members had to testify in court to disprove the accusation that real dogs were used in the making of the film. Special effects artist Carlo Rambaldi managed to save Fulci from a two-year prison sentence by presenting the fake dog props in court to an apparently disbelieving judiciary. This was the first time ever in film history that an effects artist had to prove his work was not real in a court of law.

Arty and drug fuelled, colourful and wild, hauntingly surreal, and accompanied by a groovy musical score from the legendary Ennio Morricone, *A Lizard in a Woman's Skin* is very reminiscent of an Agatha Christie-style whodunit, with some generous buckets of swinging London sleaze thrown in for good measure. It has also become something of a much-sought-after cult movie with genre fans over the years, a fact probably attributable to its often unavailability in many DVD stores.

18. Dressed To Kill

Brian De Palma's 1980 movie *Dressed To Kill* could be described as a kind of American giallo movie. All the signature elements we come to expect from your typical Italian giallo are there: eroticism and nudity, a shadowy and unknown figure using a razor to dispatch his (or her) victims, and a desperate attempt by the protagonists to unmask the crazed killer before any more horrific slayings are perpetrated.

Angie Dickinson stars as Kate Miller, a woman who is discontent in her marriage. In fact, she has become so restless in her marital misery that she even dallies with her psychiatrist, Dr Robert Elliott (Michael Caine). However, Elliott rejects her advances.

Later, at the Metropolitan Museum of Art, Kate has an unexpected flirtation with a mysterious stranger. They eventually end up outside, when Kate accompanies him in a taxi. They then start to have wild sex, and they continue this back at his apartment.

When Kate awakens some hours later, she decides to surreptitiously leave the man whilst he's sleeping. But she accidentally leaves her wedding ring on a nightstand, and when she returns to the apartment to retrieve it, she is brutally slashed to death by a tall blonde woman, in dark sunglasses, in the elevator. Call girl Liz Blake (Nancy Allen) witnesses the murder, and instantly becomes a suspect

41

herself in the eyes of the police. In an effort to clear her name, she subsequently teams up with Kate's revenge-motivated son Peter (Keith Gordon) in a desperate attempt to find the killer.

The early, and quite shocking, death of Kate in the movie is very reminiscent of Janet Leigh's similar demise in *Psycho*. In fact, De Palma does seem to pay a big homage to Hitchcock's timeless thriller in the making of this film. Moreover, you did see similar nods to Hitchcock in many of De Palma's other movies like, for example, *Sisters* and *Obsession*.

All in all, *Dressed To Kill* manages to pull off being quite a classy and rather sleazy movie at the same time, thanks to the consummate directing skills of De Palma. Also, the brilliant acting of Angie Dickinson, Michael Caine and Nancy Allen enhance the movie's appeal to a most satisfactory extent. Certainly one to add to your giallo collection.

19. Death Carries A Cane

Death Carries a Cane (Italian title: *Passi di danza su una lama di rasoio/ Dance Steps on the Edge of a Razor*), is a 1973 Italian giallo film directed by Maurizio Pradeaux. It starred Robert Hoffmann, Nieves Navarro and Luciano Rossi. It was later released on video as *The Tormentor, Maniac at Large, The Night of the Rolling Heads* and *Devil Blade*.

Kitty (Susan Scott), a photographer, witnesses the brutal killing of a woman through the window of a nearby house whilst peering through a tourist telescope. Unable to get a good view of the killer's face, she does however notice one distinguishing factor: the murderer walks with a cane. She reports the incident to the police. It is not long before other witnesses who saw the killer flee are brutally murdered. We eventually learn that the murders have some connection with the dance business. Will Kitty be the next victim?

Death Carries A Cane is a pretty average giallo, and did not really grab me as much as movies like *Deep Red* or *The Bird With The Crystal Plumage* did. However, having said that, the film does have its moments, with some pretty good murder set pieces, and more than enough to keep the typical giallo buff satisfied. There are also some generous dollops of nudity thrown in for good measure. And the opening is very reminiscent of Hitchcock's *Rear Window*. In regard to the ending, well, without giving too much away, let's just say that it could have been a little better thought out.

In conclusion, *Death Carries A Cane* is a fairly suitable watch to while away a rainy Sunday afternoon. But don't expect too many jaw-dropping, memorable moments from this movie, as it does fall a little short of being the kind of classic giallo flick you can go back to again and again.

20. The Black Belly of the Tarantula

The Black Belly of the Tarantula is a 1971 giallo movie directed by Paolo Cavara and produced by Marcello Danon. The film does share some similarities with Dario Argento's masterpiece *The Bird With The Crystal Plumage* in its style, although it's not quite as entertaining and gripping, being instead a pretty average giallo.

Short in Rome and with stunning cinematography, the storyline revolves around a mysterious killer, who is attacking women that have links with a blackmail conspiracy. Wearing a pair of surgical gloves, the crazed murderer slaughters his victims by, firstly, paralysing them with a needle before slicing open their stomachs (which is similar to the way tarantulas are killed by black or spider wasps) with a sharp knife. The horrifying thing about all of this is that the victims are fully conscious throughout their ordeal and feel no pain, but are unable to move or scream.

Inspector Tellini (Giancarlo Giannini) is assigned to investigate these serial crimes. As suspects keep getting murdered, the inspector focuses his attention on a spa, which all the victims had a connection with.

The movie also stars three Bond girls: Claudine Auger (*Thunderball, Twitch of the Death Nerve*), Barbara Bouchet (*Casino Royale, Don't Torture A Duckling*) and Barbara

Bach (*The Spy Who Loved Me, Short Night of the Glass Dolls*). It is a typical example of how the giallo presents the familiar kind of scenario around the drama: a world all ultra-modern and stylishly fashionable, populated by all kinds of beautiful people, but with all manner of warped tendencies and malevolent evil lurking beneath that glossy surface. When it comes to suggesting that everything in the high-life garden is NOT as rosy as we would like to think, nothing does it better than a giallo flick of this kind.

21. The New York Ripper

Truly one of the most shocking and controversial movies ever made, Lucio Fulci's 1982 slasher *The New York Ripper* (original title *Lo squartatore di New York*) tells the story of a washed-out New York cop (Jack Hedley), who joins forces with a college psychoanalyst (Almanta Keller) in an effort to track down a brutal serial killer who is indiscriminately stalking and slaughtering young women all over Manhattan.

The only clue to the sadistic killer's identity is a series of taunting phone calls from him, couched in a quacking Donald Duck-type of voice, a characteristic that has incurred more than its fair share of criticism and head-scratching questioning from many genre fans.

In true Fulci and Italian giallo style, the movie is sleazy, bloody, gritty and mercilessly violent. Indeed, many Fulci fans regard *The New York Ripper* as his darkest, most mean-spirited work. The movie does a great job in combining the police procedural giallo with the slasher sub genre, and all the kills are taken to a most graphic and perturbing extent. There are also quite a few elements of sexual perversion peppered throughout the film (including a rather notorious foot scene). And as far as the murders are concerned, well, punches certainly are not pulled as the female victims are torn, ripped, mutilated and cut up in the most disgusting, heinous ways you could possibly imagine.

So if you don't have a particularly strong stomach for real in-your-face blood and guts, then you have been warned!

In some ways, given its dark grittiness, *The New York Ripper* is reminiscent of Martin Scorseses's *Taxi Driver*, minus the social critique. In addition, the credibility of some of the actions of Jack Hedley's police detective character comes into question, as he is not only depicted chain smoking in a morgue, but he is also shown in an intimate relationship with a prostitute. Hmmm, very dodgy stuff there. And, as is blatantly obvious, Hedley's voice is dubbed into an American accent, something that I found a little jarring, considering how accustomed I have grown to Hedley's normally British diction.

The movie has been subjected to many cuts, especially by the British Board of Film Censors, since its release, and indeed was unavailable in Britain for many years. In fact, one British critic described the movie as "the most damaging film I have ever seen in my whole life". In the United States, the film received a limited theatrical release in 1984, and was released on VHS in 1987.

It's not surprising that the movie has attracted some degree of distaste in its time, for some critics have regarded it as having a rather misogynistic undercurrent running through it, in view of the extremely graphic and cold-blooded way all the female victims of the psychopath are killed. Violence against innocent, defenceless women really is at its most unparalleled here.

Although *The New York Ripper* is certainly not one of my all-time favourite giallo movies, and not one I am inclined to rewatch again and again, it does have its moments, and did hold my attention right to the very end. The cinematography is excellent, as is the acting by all the lead players. And the film is certainly awash with plenty of bloody and graphic killings, over-the-top sex scenes, not to mention a real nut job of a serial killer, who has given a whole new, darker meaning to the comparatively kiddie-tame character of Donald Duck simply by opening his gob and feigning the Disney character's voice over the phone. It is also a movie peopled with mostly irredeemable characters, topped by a rather bleak ending.

On the 25th June 2019, a 3-disc Special Limited Edition of *The New York Ripper* was released by Blue Underground. Boasting a new 4K restoration and coming in a gorgeous lenticular slipcase, this edition also offers a wealth of special features guaranteed to delight all die-hard fans of this movie.

Even after all these years, *The New York Ripper* is still a pretty tough watch if you are on the squeamish side. However, if you a real, ardent, unshockable giallo buff, and you like your slasher movies to be no-holds-barred gore fests, then this film is an absolute classic that you will gladly return to again and again.

Author's Note

If you enjoyed this book and would like to be kept up to date with all my latest releases, you can sign up for my Newsletter at: http://www.alantoner.com/subscribe-to-my-newsletter/

I would also really appreciate it if you could leave a review for this book on Amazon.

Thanks.

Alan Toner
www.alantoner.com

Printed in Great Britain
by Amazon

36764774R00036